Copyright © 2021 by Blue Powhatan Publishing Co.

All rights reserved. No part of this book may be reproduced or used in any manner without written permission of the copyright owner except for the use of quotations in a book review.

For more information, please contact
bluepowhatanpublishingco@gmail.com

FIRST EDITION

www.bluepowhatanpublishing.com

52 WEEKS
OF DRAWING PROMPTS

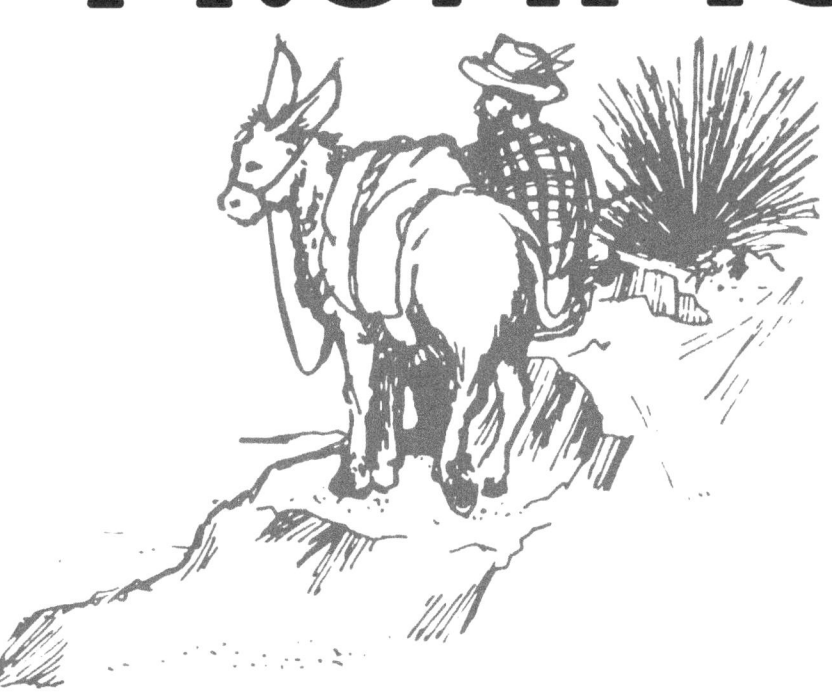

**BLUE POWHATAN
PUBLISHING CO**

"For the things we have to learn before we can do them, we learn by doing them."
- Aristotle

"Practice makes perfect. After a long time of practicing, our work will become natural, skillful, swift, and steady."
- Bruce Lee

Thank you for purchasing this year-long sketch prompt book. Unlike other prompt books, which often feature daily prompts, we believe spending time over the course of a full week on one piece can have a greater impact on progress. Take your time on each practice prompt, and feel free to skip around; no need to follow prompts in order. Do what feels best!

Now get to it!

WEEK 1
A TEENAGE COUPLE, IN A CONVERTIBLE, AT A DRIVE-IN

PRACTICE HERE, THEN
FINALIZE ON FACING PAGE

WEEK 2
CARTOON: HOUSEWIFE IN AN APRON CHASING AWAY A FOX

PRACTICE HERE, THEN
FINALIZE ON FACING PAGE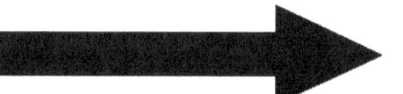

WEEK 3
A MAN IN A SUIT, SEATED AT A BUS STOP

PRACTICE HERE, THEN
FINALIZE ON FACING PAGE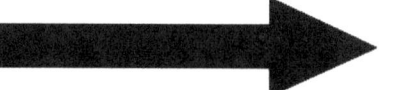

WEEK 4
AN EMPTY ROOM WITH ONE WINDOW, AND A CITYSCAPE BEYOND

PRACTICE HERE, THEN
FINALIZE ON FACING PAGE

WEEK 5
A GREAT HORNED OWL

PRACTICE HERE, THEN FINALIZE ON FACING PAGE

WEEK 6
STILL LIFE: AN OPEN, WORN MAILBOX

PRACTICE HERE, THEN FINALIZE ON FACING PAGE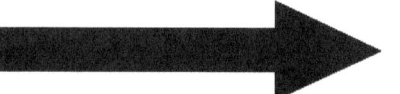

WEEK 7
A FROG JUMPING MID-AIR, GRABBING A FLY

PRACTICE HERE, THEN
FINALIZE ON FACING PAGE

WEEK 8
HAND LETTERING PRACTICE: DRAW THE PHRASE "MERRY CHRISTMAS" IN SCRIPT WITH FLOUISHES

PRACTICE HERE, THEN FINALIZE ON FACING PAGE

WEEK 9
A COFFEE SHOP SCENCE, VIEWED THROUGH STREET WINDOW

22 PRACTICE HERE, THEN
FINALIZE ON FACING PAGE

WEEK 10
CIRCULAR RADIAL MANDALA

PRACTICE HERE, THEN
FINALIZE ON FACING PAGE

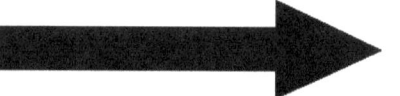

WEEK 11
SHADE PRACTICE: HARSHLY LIT WRAPPED GIFT ON WOODEN TABLE

WEEK 12
FILL THE DRAWING SPACE WITH ABSTRACT, 2-D SHAPES

PRACTICE HERE, THEN
FINALIZE ON FACING PAGE

WEEK 13
FIND AN INTERESTING PICASSO PIECE ONLINE AND RECREATE

PRACTICE HERE, THEN
FINALIZE ON FACING PAGE

WEEK 14
CLOSEUP OF A LIT CANDLE IN A DARK ROOM

PRACTICE HERE, THEN FINALIZE ON FACING PAGE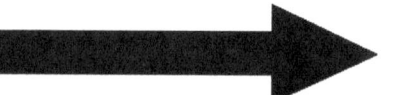

WEEK 15
A LANDSCAPE, BUT WITH LAND FEATURES (MOUNTAINS, TREES) IN TOTAL SILHOUETTE SO THAT DETAIL FOCUS IS ONLY ON SKY & CLOUDS

PRACTICE HERE, THEN
FINALIZE ON FACING PAGE

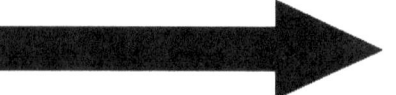

WEEK 16
AN EMPTY HIGHWAY WITH ADJACENT POWERLINES

PRACTICE HERE, THEN
FINALIZE ON FACING PAGE

WEEK 17
A FAMILY OF DUCKS WALKING IN LINE TOWARD A WATER BODY

PRACTICE HERE, THEN
FINALIZE ON FACING PAGE

WEEK 18
LETTERING PRACTICE: FIT WORDS "WORK HARDER" INSIDE A SILHOUETTED TOOL OF YOUR CHOICE

PRACTICE HERE, THEN FINALIZE ON FACING PAGE

WEEK 19
LAKE, SURROUNDED BY MOUNTAINS, AT NIGHT

PRACTICE HERE, THEN
FINALIZE ON FACING PAGE

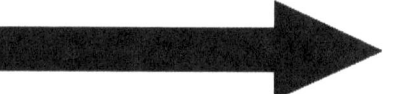

WEEK 20
STILL LIFE: HIGHLY REFLECTIVE SPOON, RESTING ON TABLE

PRACTICE HERE, THEN
FINALIZE ON FACING PAGE

WEEK 21
AMPERSANDS: IN AT LEAST TEN UNIQUE VARIATIONS

PRACTICE HERE, THEN
FINALIZE ON FACING PAGE

WEEK 22
A FLOWING SCROLL BANNER WRAPPED AROUND A SWORD

PRACTICE HERE, THEN
FINALIZE ON FACING PAGE

> # WEEK 23
> # AN ANDROID ROBOT, ARMS CROSSED, BY A BRICK WALL

PRACTICE HERE, THEN FINALIZE ON FACING PAGE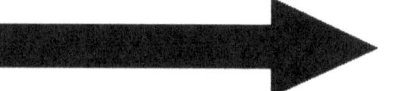

WEEK 24
RECREATE THE ICONIC ROSIE THE RIVETER, WITH A CREATIVE SPIN OF YOUR CHOOSING

PRACTICE HERE, THEN
FINALIZE ON FACING PAGE

WEEK 25
VINTAGE TRUCK ON AN EMPTY DESERT ROAD

PRACTICE HERE, THEN
FINALIZE ON FACING PAGE

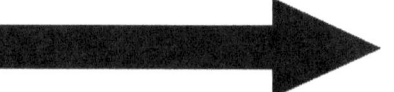

WEEK 26
AN ANTHROPOMORPHIC HARDCOVER BOOK

PRACTICE HERE, THEN
FINALIZE ON FACING PAGE

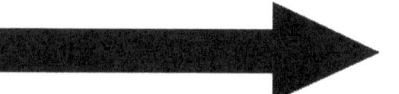

WEEK 27
A BIRD'S FEATHER, IN TEN UNIQUE VARIATIONS

PRACTICE HERE, THEN
FINALIZE ON FACING PAGE

WEEK 28
STILL LIFE: EMPTY PICTURE FRAME

PRACTICE HERE, THEN FINALIZE ON FACING PAGE

WEEK 29
A SINGLE FLOWER IN A WATER-FILLED GLASS VASE

PRACTICE HERE, THEN
FINALIZE ON FACING PAGE

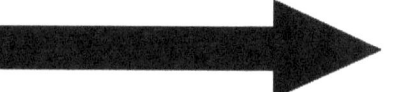

WEEK 30
A POISON DART FROG ON A LEAF

64 PRACTICE HERE, THEN
FINALIZE ON FACING PAGE

WEEK 31
STILL LIFE: A SINGLE LEATHER WORKBOOT

PRACTICE HERE, THEN
FINALIZE ON FACING PAGE

WEEK 32
A GIRL AND HER MOTHER, FISHING BY A SMALL POND

PRACTICE HERE, THEN
FINALIZE ON FACING PAGE

WEEK 33
HAND LETTERING PRACTICE: STYLIZED WORD "BELIEVE"

PRACTICE HERE, THEN FINALIZE ON FACING PAGE

WEEK 34
A WOLF CHASING A MOOSE IN THE SNOW

PRACTICE HERE, THEN
FINALIZE ON FACING PAGE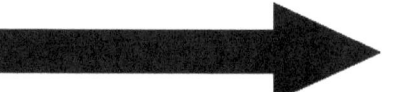

WEEK 35
STILL LIFE: AN UPRIGHT PIANO

74   **PRACTICE HERE, THEN FINALIZE ON FACING PAGE**

WEEK 36
HAND LETTERING PRACTICE: STYLIZED SCRIPT WORD "EXPLORE"

PRACTICE HERE, THEN FINALIZE ON FACING PAGE

WEEK 37
CITY STREET & BUILDINGS, AS SEEN FROM A HIGH RISE WINDOW

PRACTICE HERE, THEN FINALIZE ON FACING PAGE

WEEK 38
HAND LETTERING PRACTICE: DRAW THE PHRASE "THIS IS OUR TIME"

PRACTICE HERE, THEN FINALIZE ON FACING PAGE

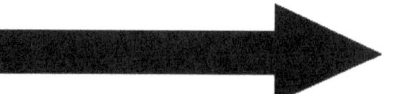

WEEK 39
A LEAFLESS DECIDUOUS TREE

82 PRACTICE HERE, THEN
FINALIZE ON FACING PAGE

WEEK 40
HAND LETTERING PRACTICE: STYLIZED WORD "FAMILY"

PRACTICE HERE, THEN FINALIZE ON FACING PAGE

WEEK 41
AN AIRPLANE COASTING THROUGH CLOUDS

86 **PRACTICE HERE, THEN FINALIZE ON FACING PAGE**

WEEK 42
A MIRRORED, STYLIZED DRAGONFLY

PRACTICE HERE, THEN FINALIZE ON FACING PAGE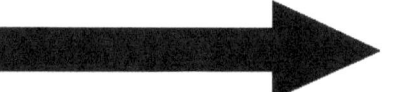

WEEK 43
LETTERING PRACTICE: NUMBERS 1-10, EACH IN A UNIQUE STYLE

PRACTICE HERE, THEN
FINALIZE ON FACING PAGE

WEEK 44
YOUR NON-DOMINANT HAND, AT REST ON A TABLE

PRACTICE HERE, THEN
FINALIZE ON FACING PAGE

WEEK 45
AN ORNATE GRANDFATHER CLOCK

PRACTICE HERE, THEN
FINALIZE ON FACING PAGE

WEEK 46
HIGH-DETAIL MAPLE LEAF

96   **PRACTICE HERE, THEN FINALIZE ON FACING PAGE**

WEEK 47
AN OLD PAYPHONE STAND, WITH RECEIVER OFF HOOK & HANGING

PRACTICE HERE, THEN
FINALIZE ON FACING PAGE

WEEK 48
STILL LIFE:
AN ABANDONED OLD SCHOOL BUS

100 **PRACTICE HERE, THEN
FINALIZE ON FACING PAGE**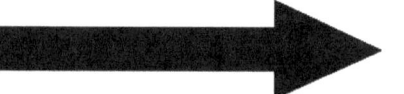

WEEK 49
CHOOSE A CHARACTER FROM ALICE IN WONDERLAND

PRACTICE HERE, THEN
FINALIZE ON FACING PAGE

WEEK 50
A CARTOON SUN, WITH A FACE AND AN INTERESTING CORONA

PRACTICE HERE, THEN
FINALIZE ON FACING PAGE

WEEK 51
MEN AND WOMEN ON BAR STOOLS, SEATED AT BAR, FROM BEHIND

PRACTICE HERE, THEN
FINALIZE ON FACING PAGE

WEEK 52
CHARICATURE ILLUSTRATION: A BEAR DRIVING A TRACTOR

PRACTICE HERE, THEN
FINALIZE ON FACING PAGE

You did it!

Thanks for joining us for this 52-week practical application of sketch prompts. Remember to *always save and date* your sketch books and practice, for progress comparison in the future

To see more of what we have available for drawing, coloring and mindfulness, visit us on Amazon at Blue Powhatan Publishing Co.

www.ingramcontent.com/pod-product-compliance
Lightning Source LLC
Chambersburg PA
CBHW060423220526
45465CB00008B/2987